Published by Creative Paperbacks
123 South Broad Street, Mankato, Minnesota 56001
Creative Paperbacks is an imprint of The Creative Company

Designed by Stephanie Blumenthal

Photographs by: GeoIMAGERY, Peter Arnold Inc., and Tom Stack & Associates

ISBN 0-89812-321-6
Library of Congress Number 00-101906

First Paperback Edition

2 4 6 8 9 7 5 3 1

SNAKE

F A C T

The sidewinder lives in deserts below sea level, the Himalayan pit viper lives atop mountains 16,000 feet (4.8 km) high, and some marine snakes never leave the sea.

Right, sidewinder; center, western diamondback scales

SNAKES AS REPTILES

Snakes are long, slender, limbless **reptiles**. These animals are very unique because instead of fur like **mammals**, moist skin like **amphibians**, or feathers like birds, reptiles have dry skin with scales.

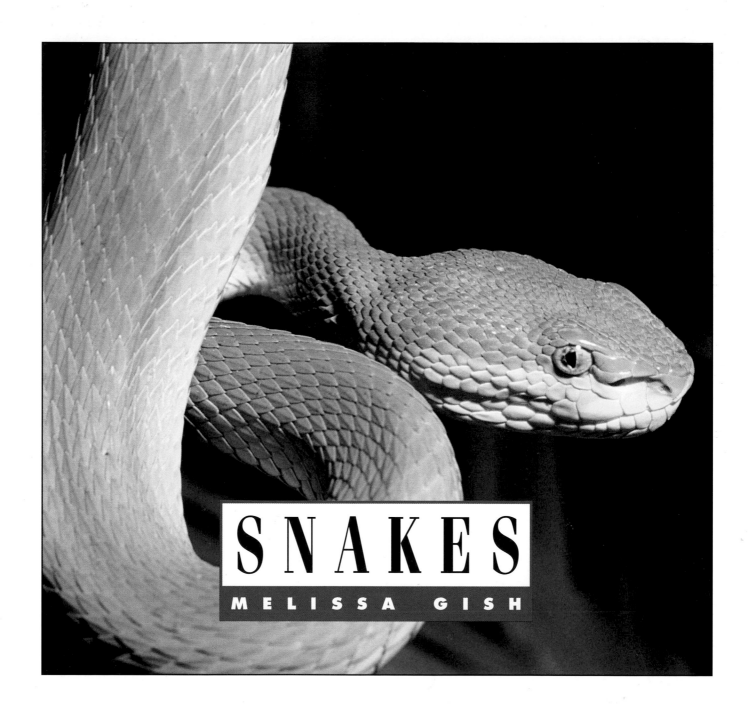

SNAKES
MELISSA GISH

CREATIVE PAPERBACKS

As the snake grows, its scales simply dry up and new, larger scales emerge. The snake then crawls out of its old skin. This process, called ecdysis, occurs about three times a year.

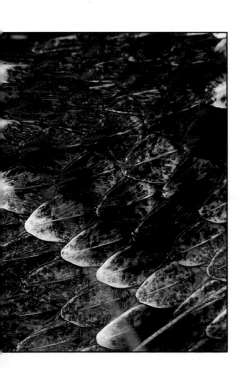

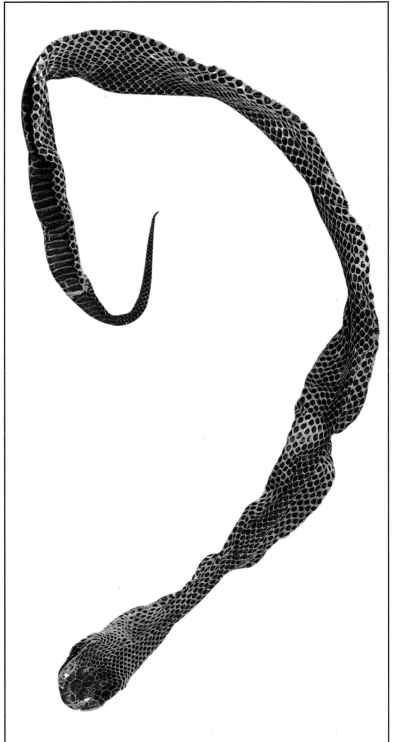

Sea snakes may look fierce—with strong bodies, oarlike tails, and large nostrils on top of the snout—and their venom is toxic, but most species are very docile.

Left, skin of a cottonmouth

SNAKE
RECORDS

The reticulated python is the longest snake in the world, reaching lengths of up to 33 feet (10 m), while the Texas blind snake, one of the world's smallest, grows to only five inches (12.7 cm) long.

Above, Texas blind snake; center, close view of a bushmaster

Another trait that sets snakes apart as reptiles is that they are **cold-blooded**. This means that their body temperature changes with the temperature around them. A snake will move in and out of the sun's rays to regulate its body temperature.

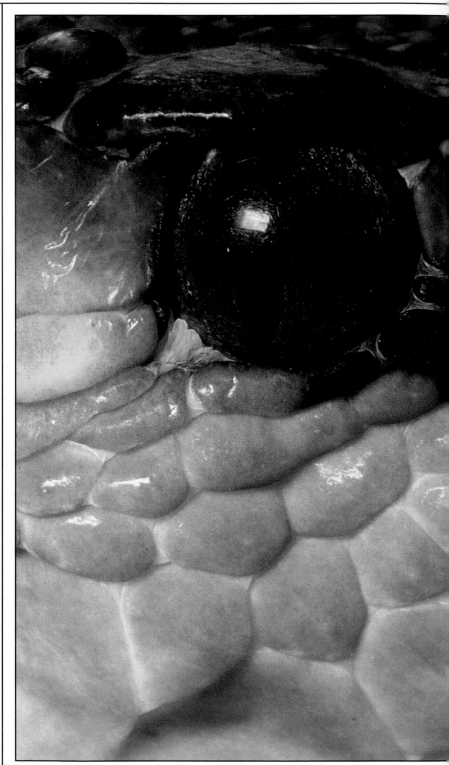

The eyes of a snake are also unusual because they cannot blink. Snakes seem to stare, and while you might think that a snake's eyes are always open, they are really always closed. That's because a clear protective membrane called a specta-cle is fused over the lens of each eye.

SNAKE
SNACK

Sea snakes are a favorite food in Japan. The meat is smoked and eaten with soy sauce.

Below, diver with a sea snake

SNAKE

SUNGLASSES

Some sun-loving snakes have yellow-tinted lenses to reduce the glare of direct sunlight.

Above, the eye of a Wagler's viper; center, blue racer

HOW SNAKES HUNT

All snakes are **carnivorous**. This means they eat such animals as mice, birds, fish, frogs, worms, insects, and even other snakes.

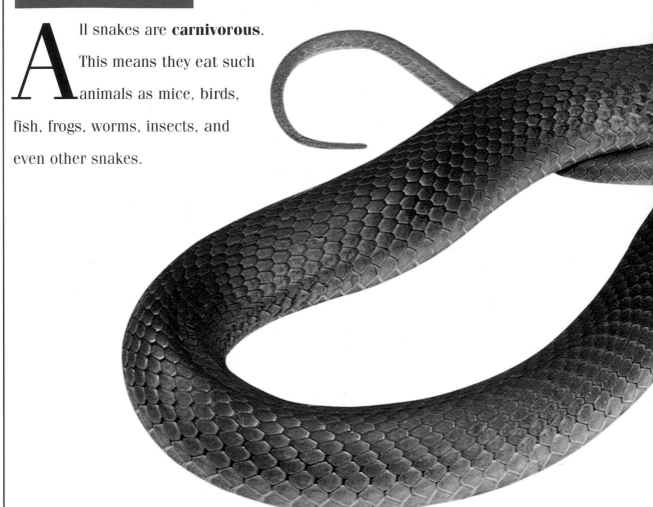

Snakes can see movement, but their distance vision is poor, so they don't use their eyes to hunt for **prey**. They don't have ears, so they cannot listen for their next meal, either. One way they do hunt is by using small bones in their heads called **columella** to feel sound vibrations.

The hognose snake
has a broad nose
that is used like a
shovel for digging.

*Left, boa constrictor
with prey; below, hog-
nose snake*

D ifferent kinds of snakes attack prey in different ways. **Constrictors** squeeze and **suffocate** their prey before swallowing it. **Venomous** snakes poison their prey and wait for it to die before eating it. Other species, such as garter snakes, seize and swallow their prey alive.

SNAKE
F A C T

The bushmaster, the longest member of the pit viper group, can reach lengths of up to 12 feet (3.6 m) and have fangs more than one inch (2.5 cm) long.

Above, egg-eating snake; top right, timber rattlesnake; bottom right, Gaboon viper with prey

HOW SNAKES EAT

Snakes don't chew their food like many other kinds of animals. They have jaws made especially for swallowing prey whole. The lower jaw is actually two halves that can be rotated or moved apart. Also, the entire lower jaw can disconnect from the upper jaw. This allows some snakes to swallow food as wide as their own heads.

Swallowing prey can take hours, so snakes have windpipes that can move forward over the tongue. This will allow a snake to still breathe while it's eating.

SNAKE VENOM

Most snakes have small teeth that are used to push food into their throats, but some also have a pair of sharp fangs in their upper jaw. These fangs are used for one reason: to inject poisonous **venom** into their victims. Fangs are a sign of a dangerous snake.

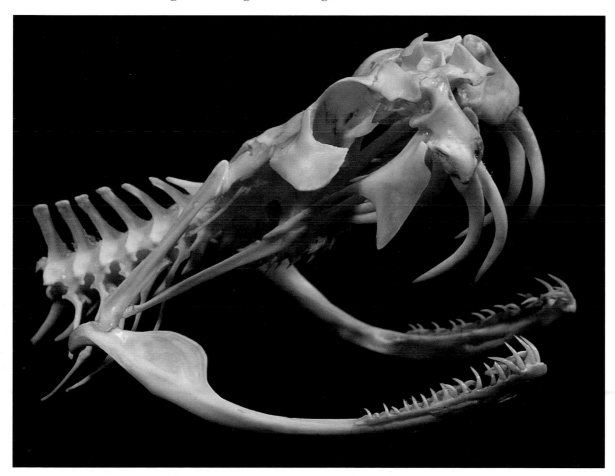

SNAKE
F A C T

The anaconda, at up to 25 feet (7.6 m), is the largest species in the boa family. It can swallow small monkeys whole.

A few species of snakes have fangs in the back of the mouth. These fangs are grooved to carry the venom that spills from **glands** inside the snake's mouth. Usually these "back-fanged" snakes are not a danger to humans, but some, such as the Southern African boomslang, can pose a threat.

Most fanged snakes are recognized by having their fangs in the front of the mouth. These fangs are shaped like hollow, slender, sharp tubes. Many of these "front-fanged" snakes, such as rattlesnakes, can fold their fangs back along the roof of the mouth. This type of fang can grow to be very large and is characteristic of snakes that have very potent venom.

Far left, anaconda; left, cottonmouth; this page, drawing venom from an eastern diamondback

SNAKE

FACT

The fangs of a rattle-snake are normally replaced two to four times a year by new fangs moving forward in the mouth. The old fangs simply fall out.

SNAKE

STOMACHS

Snakes have power-ful digestive juices, called enzymes, that completely dissolve prey, including fur, feathers, and even the bones.

Black mamba

Snake venom is secreted by special glands in the snake's mouth. Venom can cause damage to the body tissue of bite victims. Some venom contains poisonous chemicals that either **paralyze** a victim or destroy the **blood corpuscles**. This leads to the victim bleeding to death, often slowly, while its destroyed blood is still in its body.

SNAKE
HISTORY

2,000 years ago, Cleopatra, the queen of Egypt, committed suicide by allowing an Egyptian cobra to bite her.

Above, Egyptian banded cobra; right, wandering garter snake

Whenever snakes bite prey or even people, they normally do so because they are hungry or frightened. Unless hunting for food or defending their young, most snakes will attempt to avoid contact with people or other large animals.

Not all snakes are dangerous, though. Many species, such as garter snakes and some North American tree snakes, are no threat to humans. In fact, if in a proper environment, like a zoo, all snakes, including the fanged ones, are safe to observe.

There are four basic ways that you might see a snake move its body. They are called concertina movement, lateral undulation, sidewinding, and rectilinear movement.

Concertina movement is when a snake anchors the scales on the front of its body to the ground and uses its muscles to pull or drag the rest of its body behind it. It then anchors the scales on the back part of its body while it moves the front of its body forward.

SNAKE
COSTUME

The venomous Indian cobra normally flees from humans, but if it gets cornered it will rear up the front of its body, spread its foremost ribs, and extend the skin of its neck. This forms a hood that warns attackers of the snake's plan to bite.

Left, sidewinder; above, monocled cobra

SNAKE

FACT

*Snakes in the boa family are good tree climbers. These **alluvial** snakes spend little time on the ground.*

Above, tree boa on a banana plant; center, speckled rattlesnake

A snake moves with lateral undulation when it curves itself and uses the scales on the sides of its body to push against objects like rocks or grass.

A few snake species move by sidewinding. To do this, a snake loops its body into an S-shape and pushes itself sideways. This movement is perfect for travel over soft surfaces like sand.

Boas and rattle-snakes travel by rectilinear movement. They slide their skin back and forth over their muscles, forcing the **friction** of their scales against the ground or a tree to push their bodies forward.

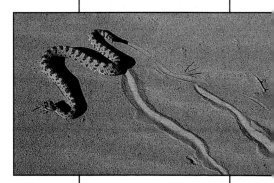

Above, Mohave Desert sidewinder

SNAKE

At up to eight feet in length (2.4 m), the eastern diamondback rattlesnake is the longest venomous snake in the U.S.

22

Above, diamondback rattlesnake; right, hognose snake emerging from its egg

SNAKE REPRODUCTION

Many snake species lay groups of eggs, or clutches, in nests, but some types of snakes can give birth to their young in much the same way that dogs and cats give birth. The number of young depends on the size and species of the snake. Pythons, for example, may lay as many as 100 eggs, and some types of vipers may give birth to more than 80 babies. Most other clutches, however, range from five to 50 young.

SNAKE
HEATER

Many types of cobras and pythons incubate their eggs. The adult will contract its muscles to raise its body temperature more than 13° F (7° C) above normal.

Left, everglades rat snakes hatching; above, a young king cobra

When the young snakes hatch from eggs weeks after being laid, they are described as oviparous. These baby snakes, such as pythons and cobras, escape their shells by using an egg tooth to break out. Since this is the only use of the egg tooth, it falls off shortly after the snakes hatch.

There are also certain types of vipers and adders whose young hatch as soon as the eggs are laid. These snakes are described as ovoviviparous.

SNAKE

Some pythons that have been born and raised in captivity have been known to live for more than 20 years.

Above, ball python, having just swallowed a mouse; right, monocled cobra hatching

Viviparous snakes develop within sacks inside their mothers' bodies and are born alive. Rattlesnakes give birth this way and deliver between 8 and 15 young at a time. Garter snakes and a rattlesnake relative called the fer-de-lance deliver as many as 70 babies at once.

All snakes, regardless of their species, normally don't care for their young or teach them how to survive. Once the babies hatch or are born, they are on their own to learn how to hunt and how to protect themselves from their many predators.

Fer-de-lance is a French-Creole word meaning "head of a lance." A lance is a sharp spear, which is just what the head of a fer-de-lance snake looks like.

SNAKE
SECRET

The earth snake is highly secretive and almost always remains in hiding beneath logs and rocks. It eats worms and soft-bodied insects.

Above, rough earth snake; center, northern copperhead

HOW SNAKES PROTECT THEMSELVES

All snakes, both young and adult, are constantly at risk of becoming a predator's next meal. Some snakes have remarkable protection and defense features against the birds, larger mammals, and even other snakes that try to eat them.

One defense feature that most snakes rely on is **camouflage**, or the ability to blend in with their environment. For example, the green boa is colored to resemble the rain forest.

SNAKE

ACTOR

When threatened, the docile hognose will play dead by rolling over onto its back and hanging its tongue out of the corner of its mouth.

Above, hognose snake playing dead

SNAKE

FACT

Sea snakes find safety in numbers, grouping together by the thousands to bask in the sun while floating on the ocean surface.

Some snakes take a bolder approach to defense. The coral snake's bright colors make it easily recognizable to predators as a highly poisonous meal.

Above, turtle-headed sea snake; right, western coral snake

The ground-dwelling eastern diamondback rattlesnake isn't afraid to face its enemies. It warns would-be attackers with a menacing rattle sound of its tail.

R egardless of the type of snake, you can be sure it has some clever way to protect itself from enemies. It's a good thing, too, because predators are not the only threat to these reptiles.

SNAKE
F A C T

The rattlesnake has a cap on the tip of its tail that catches a ring of dry skin each time the snake sheds. The rattle sound comes from the rings of dry scales rubbing against each other.

Rattlesnake rattle

30

Top right, San Francisco garter snake; bottom right, fer-de-lance; far right, golden cape cobra

DANGERS TO SNAKES

Fewer than 1,000 of the nearly 3,000 species of snakes in the world are poisonous, and less than 300 can be fatal to humans. Unfortunately, humans can be fatal to snakes as well. **Habitat** destruction and poisoning has threatened many snake species with **extinction**. The Indian python, once abundant in India and Sri Lanka, is now **endangered**, as are the San Francisco garter snake and the eastern indigo snake of the United States.

Not only do snakes serve as food for other larger animals, but their own eating habits help balance the populations of their prey. They are a valuable part of the world's **ecosystem** and are beautiful and fascinating animals. We should all take the time to understand the important roles that snakes play in nature.

Glossary

Alluvial animals spend most of their time in trees high above the ground.

Amphibians are animals with gills that breathe water when young but breathe air and live in or near water as adults.

Blood corpuscles are the living blood cells that grow in a human or animal body.

Camouflage is a way of hiding from danger by appearing to be part of the environment.

A **carnivorous** animal survives on a diet consisting of the meat of other animals.

A **cold-blooded** animal relies on its environment to help regulate its body temperature.

The **columella** is the bony rod inside a reptile's ear that detects sound vibrations.

Constrictors are snakes that squeeze their prey to death before eating it.

An **ecosystem** is a group of plants and animals living together. Ecosystems can be large, like the whole world, or very small, like a pond or forest.

Endangered animals are threatened with becoming so few in number that their kind will suffer **extinction**, dying out completely and disappearing from Earth.

Friction is the force between two objects rubbing against each other. Some snakes use this force to move their bodies.

Glands are organs that perform certain functions inside the body of a human or an animal. Bodies contain many different kinds of glands.

A **habitat** is the environment where a plant or animal naturally lives and grows.

Mammals are animals that feed their young with milk from the mother's body and whose skin is covered with hair or fur.

Some venom will **paralyze** a victim, which means its body functions no longer work and it is powerless to move.

Pit organs are the highly-developed heat sensors on the heads of some snakes; they are used for detecting prey.

Prey is the term used for any animal that becomes a meal for a carnivorous animal.

Reptiles are animals that crawl on their bellies (snakes) or on small, short legs (lizards) and whose bodies are covered with scales or bony plates.

Prey that are squeezed by constrictors **suffocate**, or are made to stop breathing.

Venom is the poison created inside the body of a **venomous** animal. Venom is used to kill prey.